THE LIBRARY OF WEAPONS OF MASS DESTRUCTION™

Nuclear Weapons
and the
Cold War

MARK BEYER

The Rosen Publishing Group, Inc., New York

Published in 2005 by The Rosen Publishing Group, Inc.
29 East 21st Street, New York, NY 10010

First Edition

Publisher Cataloging Data

Beyer, Mark (Mark T.)
Nuclear weapons and the Cold War / by Mark Beyer.
p. cm. — (The Library of weapons of mass destruction).
Includes bibliographical references and index.
Summary: This book describes the potential dangers of the Cold War and explains how the U.S. and the Soviet Union negotiated peace through arms reduction.
ISBN 1-4042-0290-0
1. Nuclear warfare—Juvenile literature. 2. Cold War—Juvenile literature. 3. Nuclear weapons—Political aspects—Juvenile literature. 4. World politics—1945–1989—Juvenile literature. 5. United States—Foreign relations—Soviet Union—Juvenile literature. 6. Soviet Union—Foreign relations—United States—Juvenile literature [1. Nuclear warfare. 2. Cold War. 3. Nuclear weapons. 4. World politics—1945– 5. United States—Foreign relations—Soviet Union. 6. Soviet Union—Foreign relations—United States]
I. Title. II. Series
2005
355.02'17–dc22

Manufactured in the United States of America

On the cover: President John F. Kennedy meets with U.S. military officials during the Cuban Missile Crisis in 1962.

[CONTENTS]

INTRODUCTION

The Cold War is a period in twentieth-century history during which the two most powerful nations, the Soviet Union and the United States, stood against each other with armies and nuclear weapons, but never went to war. Had the two nations actually fought, nuclear weapons would have surely been used and great destruction would have been seen across the world.

Historians date the Cold War from 1945 to 1990, but the seeds of this war had been planted decades before. The United States did not like the

Ever since the first such test, the Trinity Test at Alamogordo, New Mexico, in July 1945, witnesses to test explosions of nuclear weapons have been awed and terrified at the sight. This is a ground-level view of a surface test of a nuclear device in the Nevada desert on April 15, 1955.

Communist revolution that took place in Russia in 1917, and did its best to restrain Communist control and expansion. This brought tensions between the two countries right up to World War II (1939–1945). But at that time, the enemies were Adolf Hitler (1889–1945) and Nazism, and for the moment the United States and Soviet Union put their differences aside to fight together against Hitler's plan for world domination. Yet even before the war ended, the old distrust returned between the United States and the Soviet Union.

Despite the many conflicts brought on by the Cold War, the Soviet and U.S. governments were not always on the brink of battle. The Cold War was more of an ebb and flow of tensions between the two nations. By the Cold War's last decade, however, the Soviet Union was vastly overmatched in military spending, and its populace tired of strict rule after more than seventy years under Communism. After one final attempt to keep pace with the U.S. buildup of nuclear arms, the Soviets showed signs of cracking under the pressure. Finally, a change of leadership in the Soviet Union brought about ideas and policies for change. When these took hold with the public, it was really only a matter of time before the Communist system changed forever. By 1989, the Soviet Union was beginning to fall apart, and the Cold War would come to an end the following year. ■

A giant mushroom cloud rises into the atmosphere above the Japanese city of Nagasaki after the atomic bomb was dropped there on August 9, 1945. A reporter who flew with the bombers described it as "a giant pillar of purple fire . . . shooting skyward with enormous speed" topped by a mushroom cloud that was "seething and boiling in a white fury of creamy foam."

PERSPECTIVE AND HISTORY

1

The United States' invention and use of the first atomic bombs against the Japanese cities of Hiroshima and Nagasaki in 1945 painted a new picture of the world for all people. The bomb's destructive force was thought to make war—or large-scale war—impossible in the future. Its threatened use, military experts agreed, would cause any land-hungry leader to think twice before invading another country. The first enemy

to be threatened in this manner was the Soviet Union in 1946. This former ally to the United States, Great Britain, France, and others had left its armies in Eastern Europe after the end of World War II and Germany's destruction. The Soviets wanted to keep the land, the countries, and the people for their own empire created during wartime. Also, having lost more than 20 million people during WWII, the Soviet Union desired a buffer zone for its own security. The peace of post-WWII was threatened even before cities had had a chance to rebuild.

The United States and the other allies had since disbanded most of their war machines and sent their armies home. Yet each was fearful that the Soviet Union would simply—and could at this point—march west and take even more European lands if it so decided. A real threat of war was brewing, but the United States had an ace up its

Tanks from the victorious Red Army of the Soviet Union roll through the rubble of Berlin, the capital city of defeated Nazi Germany, in August 1945. Although still officially allies, the United States and the Soviet Union had begun to maneuver against each other's postwar supremacy even before the end of World War II.

sleeve: the atom bomb. In 1946, it used the threat of its small nuclear bomb arsenal to keep the Soviet army at the established borders of Poland, Czechoslovakia, Bulgaria, Romania, Hungary, and the Russian-controlled areas of Austria and Germany. The arsenal was much smaller than the Soviets thought, and the planes the United States had sent over to Germany, France, and Great Britain were in fact not the right size to effectively deliver the bombs. But the mere fact of having atomic bombs had kept the Soviets from going beyond thinking about further European conquest. The two nations—and half a continent—were at a stalemate.

Vladimir Lenin was the leader of the Communist Bolsheviks, a party that, despite its small numbers, succeeded in seizing power in the Soviet Union after the overthrow of the Russian monarchy in 1917.

In 1947, President Harry S. Truman developed a plan to contain Soviet might and movement. This plan was dubbed the Truman Doctrine and pledged to help "free peoples who are resisting attempted subjugation by armed minorities or outside pressures." The Truman Doctrine was aimed at the Soviet threat, but it would soon be used throughout the world. How had these two former allies come to this point so quickly?

SEEDS OF DISTRUST

Communist Bolsheviks led by Vladimir Lenin (1870–1924) overthrew the Russian czar Nicholas II in 1917. Lenin established a Communist government in Russia that controlled all industry, business,

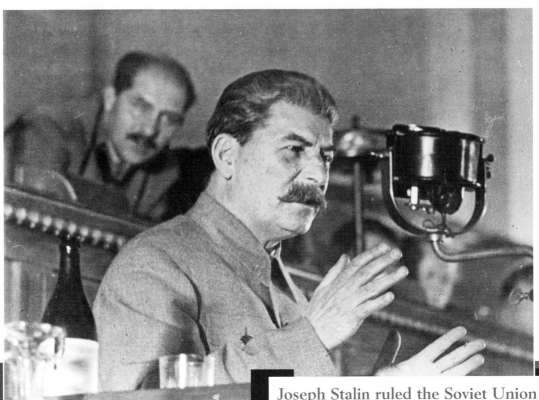

Joseph Stalin ruled the Soviet Union from 1929 to his death in 1953. During that period, Russia was transformed from a predominantly peasant nation to a major industrial power that was largely responsible for the defeat of Nazi Germany in World War II and emerged from the war as the United States' greatest rival.

and government. This type of government was opposite to that of the United States, where people elected government representatives, and private citizens and corporations owned businesses and industry. When Lenin called for all workers of the world to unite and throw off the chains of industrialist rule, the United States found its newest enemy. Communist ideas began to spread around the world, even in the United States. But Communism did not take hold in many nations just yet. Russia was the model, but its system was not quite working well for all the people to live happily as the leaders had promised.

When Lenin died in 1924, a power struggle for Russia ensued, and Joseph Stalin (1879–1953) came to power. He ruled with a brutal fist to keep power and control the country's industry, farming, and people. What the United States most feared about Communism—dictatorial control—

had quickly come true. The United States moved to crack down on its own Communist Party members and used its money and power overseas to do the same in other countries. Meanwhile, Stalin used his power and influence in Europe, through such avenues as academics, to spread the idea of Communism. Eventually, this attempt to influence countries, and the Soviet development of its own atomic bomb, would bring about the Cold War. However, despite the powerful distrust between the two countries, they needed each other's help after the rise of Hitler and the beginning of World War II.

THE ATOMIC BOMB

In 1939, with war looming over Europe for the second time in twenty years, scientists led by Albert Einstein encouraged the United States to start a nuclear program that could build an atomic bomb. No one knew exactly how powerful this bomb could or would be, but the scientists warned President Franklin Roosevelt that Hitler's own scientists were trying to build a nuclear-powered bomb.

The project was led by an agency called the Corps of Engineers' Manhattan Engineer District. The program became known as the Manhattan Project. Major General Leslie R. Groves led the project. Physicist J. Robert Oppenheimer (1904–1967) oversaw the bomb's design and construction. Research and building of the bomb took place at locations such as Los Alamos, New Mexico, and Oak Ridge, Tennessee.

Nuclear fission, or the splitting of atoms to create energy, was first tested beneath the stands of an athletic playing field at the University of Chicago. Such now-famous scientists as Enrico Fermi, Eugene Wigner, and Leo Szilard worked on this test. The test used 50 tons (45 metric tons) of natural uranium oxide and uranium surrounded by 500 tons (450 metric tons) of graphite. This combination was the nuclear pile, called the reactor. The motive for the test was to prove that a chain reaction could be made using radioactive material (uranium). On December 2, 1942, the scientists produced the first atomic chain reaction.

The product of their tests was plutonium, a highly enriched form of uranium that would be the bomb material. Plutonium is more

Oppenheimer points at a picture of the pillar and mushroom cloud rising from the explosion of the atomic bomb in the Japanese city of Hiroshima on August 6, 1945. "We knew the world would not be the same," Oppenheimer said after the Manhattan Project's first successful test of a nuclear device.

radioactive than uranium in its natural state, and when a chain reaction is forced by explosive material surrounding the plutonium, an atomic explosion occurs. At least that's what Oppenheimer and the other scientists predicted would happen. The truth was they weren't exactly sure that it would work.

Near Alamogordo, New Mexico, on July 16, 1945, they found out by testing the first nuclear bomb. Some scientists feared the chain reaction of nuclear fission could cause the entire planet to explode with its own atoms reacting to the explosion. Others considered the possibility that the bomb would be not much more destructive than those the military already had. The test produced the first nuclear-powered explosion exactly as the scientists had predicted, with the force of several tons of TNT.

The United States had enough plutonium to build two bombs. Both were used on Japanese cities to try to bring an end to World War II. Two days after the second bomb was used on Nagasaki, the Japanese surrendered. The United States then continued to build more bombs.

THE SOVIETS GET THE BOMB

By 1949, the United States had a small nuclear arsenal, mostly in Europe, to contain the new Soviet threat. The United States knew the Soviet government was conducting its own nuclear research and testing. Yet the assumption was that the Soviets were years away from having the technology to make and explode their own bomb. In September 1949, the United States air force detected unnatural levels and types of radioactivity while on a routine weather mission high above the easternmost Soviet province of Kamchatka. America's nuclear monopoly had lasted a mere four years plus one month.

President Truman didn't consider this achievement any great harm. He had quickly decided back in 1945, that nuclear weapons were such a different weapon that leaders would not be so quick to use them. The atom bomb was not very practical. It destroyed everything, and using it on each other would only cause the ruin of both countries. He couldn't

WITNESS TO DESTRUCTION

When J. Robert Oppenheimer saw what he had helped develop at the Los Alamos test explosion, he remembered a phrase from the Hindu script *Bhagavad Gita*: "Now I am become Death, the Destroyer of Worlds."

President Harry S. Truman led the United States through the first years of the Cold War. He had been in office less than four months when he made the decision to use the atomic bomb against Japan to bring an end to World War II. "[I] never had any doubt it should be used," he later wrote.

imagine any leader wanting to see his own destruction, even Stalin. Because of this fact, Truman had quickly ruled out any use of the bomb by the military without presidential approval and authority. Truman was quoted as telling his defense secretary that he would not allow a "dashing lieutenant colonel deciding when would be the proper time to drop one."

The immediate outcome of the Soviets producing nuclear weapons was dramatic, however. For many months, scientists, the military, and government officials had been discussing and debating the construction of a new type of weapon: the hydrogen bomb. Where the atomic bomb split atoms to create its energy, the hydrogen bomb combined atomic nuclei (the centers of atoms) in a process called fusion. The outcome would be a weapon producing nearly a thousand times more power than any existing nuclear weapon in the American stockpile. When officials learned of Soviet nuclear weapons control, they ordered the building of the H-bomb.

COMMUNISTS TAKE OVER CHINA

On October 1, 1949, in China, the Communist Mao Zedong proclaimed victory, ending China's civil war. The United States now worried about the politics of the world's second-largest country. The Soviets were not necessarily friendly with China's new leaders. Yet, since the country was Communist, the United States saw an automatic alliance between them. Stalin could use this fact as a basis for future help against America.

Mao, for his part, wanted to use his newfound power to influence his Asian neighbors. He wanted to spread Communism across all of Southeast Asia. In northern Korea, a Communist government already controlled its people. Communist leaders also controlled northern Vietnam and were battling the French, who had colonized much of Southeast Asia for more than a hundred years. American influence in the region was being pushed aside by a new ideology—Communism. The world's two superpowers, now both in possession of nuclear weapons, were on edge over each other's influence in different parts of the world.

THE KOREAN WAR

In early 1950, Western and Eastern Europe were divided, with America's "nuclear umbrella" holding off (or so the West thought) a Soviet advance. Just a year before, America's support of Europe's defense led to the formation of the North Atlantic Treaty Organization (NATO). NATO linked the Western European nations with America's military strength to protect

Well-disguised South Korean troops await a North Korean advance in August 1950, during the first months of the Korean War. The United States fought two major wars in Asia during the Cold War, in Korea and then in Vietnam. Today, North Korea's interest in acquiring weapons of mass destruction continues to be a major security concern and foreign policy issue for the United States.

against possible Soviet aggression. Meanwhile, northeast and southeast Asian governments were turning to Communism. The Truman Doctrine was in full swing, and America was helping any country that asked for assistance to fight the Communist threat worldwide.

This was never more evident than in Korea. In 1948, the Communist north and democratic south were split along the 38th parallel between U.S. and Soviet occupying troops. In June 1950, the North Korean army attacked the south, trying to reunite the country under Communist rule. The American government was sure that the attack was provoked by both the Soviets and Chinese urging the North Korean government (or even ordering the attack). The North Korean army almost drove the U.S. and South Korean armies off the peninsula.

The United States brought the attack to the attention of the United

General Douglas MacArthur waves to an estimated crowd of 4,500,000 people at a parade held in his honor in Chicago, Illinois, on April 26, 1951, after the general had been recalled from service in Korea. Despite his enormous popularity, MacArthur's insubordination and recklessness forced Truman to replace him as commander of the UN forces in the Korean War.

Nations Security Council, which voted to send troops from several nations, led by the United States, to push back the invading north. Usually this would have been impossible because as a Security Council member, the Soviet Union would have vetoed this action. But the Soviets had boycotted the United Nations (UN) months before.

UN troops led by General Douglas MacArthur (1880–1904), and using America's naval and air force strength, pushed the North Koreans back to the 38th parallel. MacArthur wanted to advance into China. He even wanted to use nuclear weapons. President Truman refused both ideas, but he did allow the army to advance past the 38th parallel. This set off Mao Zedong, who feared the UN troops would enter China. China sent across its border hundreds of thousands of troops in human wave attacks to battle the UN troops.

When MacArthur went public in 1951, with his demands to use the bomb against Chinese troops, Truman fired the WWII hero. Meanwhile, the Chinese troops pushed the UN forces back to the 38th parallel and the fighting continued for two more years in a war of attrition, or killing as many of the enemy as possible. The war went on in this way while an agreement to end hostilities was negotiated for the next two years.

There were few lessons from the Korean War. What stuck out most prominently, however, was the willingness on the part of both superpowers to use other countries as their Cold War battlefield.

ANTI-COMMUNISM AT HOME

Tensions between governments were brought home to everyday Americans. By the late 1940s, the Truman administration was using loyalty oaths to weed out Communist-minded Americans from positions of power within the government. Americans were being pitted against one another.

This distrust became rabid in 1950, when a Republican senator from Wisconsin, Joseph McCarthy (1908–1957), led a government inquisition to root out any Communists from every walk of life. McCarthy's first targets were former card-carrying Communists presently working in the government. He organized the Permanent Subcommittee on Investigations and used television to destroy the characters of hundreds of

Senator Joseph McCarthy uses a map of the United States to point out areas of alleged Communist Party infiltration at a Senate hearing in June 1954. The hearing was to mark the end of McCarthy's influence. When he recklessly accused the army of being "soft" on Communism, even former supporters turned away from him.

individuals. Hundreds more lost their jobs and were locked out of professions in education, the motion picture industry, and television. These were professions that had direct contact or possible influence over Americans. Many of these people had in fact been Communists, but many years earlier, when they were young. McCarthy and his cohorts did not count the time difference.

The terror of nuclear weapons was not so much on the minds of Americans in the early 1950s. The public, of course, knew that the Soviets had nuclear weapons, but they also knew, or believed, that America had many more weapons. Knowing that the military had an advantage in quantity of bombs gave people peace of mind that all-out war would be averted. In just a few years, however, the buildup of nuclear weapons between the United States and the Soviet Union would bring about the term "arms race." With so many bombs being stockpiled in the country and around the world, people began to wonder if one of the two nuclear superpowers might decide to use the weapons. So, too, did the government and military leaders in both countries. ◾

Technicians check Nike missiles at their launch site in Lorton, Virginia, in December 1954. The Nike was the world's first successful guided surface-to-air missile. It was developed as a "last-resort" aerial defense system for American population centers and other sites of strategic importance against attack by Soviet aircraft.

2

THE ARMS RACE

The Soviet Union had suffered great damage to its industry and land during WWII. It had also lost 10 percent of its population. Even eight years after the war, in 1953, the Soviet Union was still clawing its way back from industrial ruin. The government really had no money to maintain a huge military, yet it feared the United States and Western European powers, with their vast industrial capacity and strong militaries. According to the Soviet Union, the nations of the West

Newly developed Soviet SA-2 missiles are trucked by the Kremlin, the seat of the Soviet government, during a parade in Moscow commemorating the fortieth anniversary of the Bolshevik Revolution on November 7, 1957. This missile was touted as being able to reach the latest bomber plane developed by the United States and included an early warning radar.

were the threatening governments, not itself. In some ways its fears were justified. While the Soviet government was retooling its industry for farm equipment and industrial machinery to feed people and put them back to work, America and its Western European allies were amassing troops and nuclear weapons along the Eastern European borders. What could the Soviets think other than that enemy armies could invade again, just as Hitler had done in 1941?

NUCLEAR WEAPONS BUILDUP

The Soviets, therefore, looked to nuclear weapons as the future of their military strength. Atomic bombs were cheap to build and cheap to maintain. The United States Air Force was far stronger than the Soviet Union's own, but by having as many bombs as possible, Soviet leaders gambled that any attack by the West could be survived simply with an advantage of bombs to use against their enemies. Meanwhile, the Soviet government was working on a rocket program that would further eliminate the need for vast amounts of money to build jet bombers.

Naturally, the American government had its own fears. One was that Communists wanted world domination. They were seeing this in Korea and Southeast Asia. What part of the world would be next? Americans had their suspicions—for instance Latin America and Africa—and so began their own program to increase military spending. This included nuclear weapons, bombers to carry the weapons, and the making of smaller weapons to be used on the battlefield shot from cannons. The arms race had begun without further thought of the consequences.

The U.S. military tested the first hydrogen bomb in 1952. Later that year, Dwight D. Eisenhower was elected president of the United States. His leadership as supreme allied commander appealed to a nation fearful of Communist threat worldwide. Even though he had promised during his campaign to reduce military spending, Eisenhower immediately expanded military spending to build up the nuclear weapons stockpile. He, too, understood that nuclear weapons were cheap compared to the cost of maintaining troops, tanks, and ships around the world.

As president of the United States from 1952 to 1960, Dwight Eisenhower supported a strong national defense. But on leaving office, he warned Americans about the dangers of what he called the "military-industrial complex," or the vast permanent armaments industry, which he had come to see as a threat to democracy.

The United States already had hundreds of long-range jet bombers—B-52s—that flew world-wide twenty-four hours a day. The Soviets could not match this air advantage, and the United States knew this. The Soviets continued to build nuclear weapons and steadily increased production of their formerly massive army and tank battalions. Each side saw that the other was not going to slow down. Yet neither country was willing to go to war with troops and tanks, and neither was going to be the first to attack using atomic bombs. The entire world would be against that nation after what was witnessed in Japan. The possibility for any new war had indeed turned cold.

Part of this cooling came also in the form of the United States and the

The B-52 bomber was one of the United States' most important weapons in its contest for military supremacy with the Soviet Union. In an effort to keep the bomber top secret after its completion, it left the Boeing plant covered with muslin. Test flights were done at night, and all negatives of photos taken were developed at a secret location in Washington, D.C. Although the last B-52 was delivered to the military in June 1962, the huge plane remains the primary "nuclear-roled" aircraft in the U.S. military.

Soviet Union pulling back from antagonizing the other. They began to respect the lines that had been drawn in areas known as each other's spheres of influence. For the Soviets, this meant the Eastern European countries that they had controlled militarily (and now politically as well) following the end of WWII. For the United States, this meant Western Europe, the Middle East, and South America.

A DANGEROUS IDEA

Truman hadn't seen a use for atomic weapons in war. They were simply too destructive for the few skirmishes that could be foreseen. Eisenhower publicly felt the same. But as a former military commander, he understood the uselessness of a weapon that your enemy knew you wouldn't use—or couldn't, based on public opinion—or even threaten to use. So what was the point in having nuclear weapons if a country didn't use them?

MacArthur had asked this question while commanding forces in Korea. Other military commanders had been asking the same question. That's why Truman made it a policy that only the president himself could authorize their use. American leaders thought these questions out but also asked themselves if Soviet leaders saw the same uselessness of having stockpiles if they were never to be used. These were dangerous questions with world-changing consequences if one or the other country decided that using nuclear weapons was a matter of practicality in a time of war.

HOW THE COLD WAR GOT ITS NAME

Back in 1947, the journalist Walter Lippman wrote a series of articles titled "The Cold War." In them, he had illustrated the lengths at which the Soviets and America went to provoke each other just short of engaging in war. As the games that these two superpowers played against each other went on and got more dangerous—but the countries never quite came to fighting each other—the name stuck.

Then an advance in science caused a further problem in that thinking. Scientists had developed mini-sized nuclear bombs that could be shot from cannons on a battlefield. Now the use of atomic weapons could be done on a small scale. Eisenhower himself had told the UN that atomic weapons "have virtually achieved conventional status within our armed forces." Was he warning the Soviets that the United States was prepared to use atomic weapons?

STALIN DIES— AND TENSIONS EASE

Just as both countries were pouring money into their own weaponry and nuclear stock-piles, Joseph Stalin died in 1953. "Uncle Joe," as he had been called, had murdered millions and sent millions more into slave labor to help build the Soviet Union into what it was before WWII and helped to rebuild the country afterward. Most Soviet citizens were happy that Stalin was dead. The people had lived through the hardships and fear that Stalin had put them through. But they were also fearful of the future. Could someone as terrible or more so come to power? They waited.

Georgi Malenkov (1902–1988) replaced Stalin, and he wanted to give Soviet citizens a better life. He therefore moved money and industry away from the military and to social programs—farming, housing, and consumer goods.

Nikita Khrushchev proved to be far more confrontational toward the United States than Stalin had ever been. At one point, he even publicly threatened the United States, saying, "Like it or not, history is on our side. We will bury you."

Malenkov also sought better relations with the West because he wanted technical assistance that would help Soviet agriculture, hydroelectric power production, and medical advancement. Relations between the two superpowers improved. Tensions eased, though battles were still fought with other Communist governments around the globe, including the French fighting the Communist Vietcong in Vietnam, and Communist-leaning leaders such as Egypt's Gamal Nasser in the Middle East.

In 1955, Nikita Khrushchev (1894–1971) removed Malenkov from power and took control of the Soviet Union. Khrushchev didn't do anything to upset the new balance that was beginning to take hold, even though he had criticized Malenkov for being "soft" on the West. Khrushchev began what became known as the de-Stalinization of the Soviet Union. There were no more purges (arrests, imprisonment, executions) of party officials, people sent to the gulags (Soviet concentration camps), or the total fear by which people had lived under Stalin's iron-fisted rule. Khrushchev was a moderate, and he installed moderate leaders in the Soviet satellite states of Eastern Europe. Khrushchev and his government began to use the term "peaceful coexistence" when describing relations between Moscow and Washington, D.C.

THE THAW ICES OVER

Several events in the next two years quickly heated up the Cold War. First, the United States and Western European nations helped to rearm West Germany. This set the Soviets off, wondering what the Western powers could be thinking by helping the one country that had started two world wars in the twentieth century. Khrushchev responded by gathering the Soviet satellite nations and forming the Warsaw Pact in May 1955, a military alliance equal to NATO.

Next, Khrushchev moved forward with plans to build intercontinental ballistic missiles (ICBMs). These were long-range rockets that were nearly impossible to shoot down and that could deliver an atomic weapon thousands of miles in mere minutes. The United States already had short-range missiles of its own based in Western Europe.

In October 1956, the Polish and Hungarian governments revolted against their Soviet leaders. They wanted to reform their countries and

Rubble in the streets of the capital city of Budapest in November 1956 is evidence of the sad fate of the Hungarian uprising against the Soviet Union a month earlier. Despite its confrontational stance toward the Soviet Union, the United States provided no help to Hungary, which had requested aid.

move away from Communist control. People demonstrated in the streets. Hungary announced its withdrawal from the Warsaw Pact. For a few days, Khrushchev and his advisers argued about what to do. On November 4, their response came in the form of Soviet tanks and troops storming into Budapest, Hungary. Nearly 2,000 Hungarian citizens died. Another 200,000 left the country in a panic. The Hungarian premier Imre Nagy was arrested and later executed after a secret trial.

WESTERN RESPONSE

Western Europeans were shaken by the Soviet invasion of Hungary. They were furious over the murder of people just because they wanted to have more freedoms. Thousands of European Communists broke away from Soviet-style Communism and strong-arm tactics. This was not the peaceful means toward Communism that Western Communists thought was possible.

Meanwhile, the United States was almost silent about the invasion, killings, and arrests. It was more worried about the Middle East's problems with the Suez Canal, the major conduit for trade between the West, the Middle East, and the Far East, that Nasser had taken over with the Egyptian military. The United States was worried that Nasser was becoming close with Moscow. If that happened, the nations of the Middle East and their oil resources could be in jeopardy if Moscow could influence Arab rulers. Within a year, worry over Soviet satellite nations would be overshadowed by a much greater threat.

THE ROCKET-POWERED COLD WAR

In 1957, both the Soviet Union and the United States had medium-range rockets that carried nuclear bombs. The United States had these rockets at bases in Great Britain, Italy, and Turkey. They could easily reach the Soviet Union. And while the Soviets' rockets could also reach across Europe, their missiles could not harm the United States mainland. This tit-for-tat military standoff strategy changed completely in October 1957.

The launch of *Sputnik 1*, the Soviet space satellite that emitted an electronic pulse for every scientist to hear and verify, was the first successful

This is *Sputnik I,* the first artificial satellite. It orbited Earth in only ninety-eight minutes. Although it was only about the size of a basketball and weighed just 183 pounds (83 kg), *Sputnik I* introduced a whole new element to the Cold War and the arms race when it was launched in October 1957, transporting the arms race into space.

test of an ICBM. The Soviets were well on their way to developing a rocket that could be fired from their own soil and hit targets in the United States. This was not just a huge scientific advantage but Khrushchev's greatest propaganda tool. He pronounced this success as proof that Communism was the future of the world and that capitalism was all about money and decadence. The world waited for America's response, but it was mute on the subject. It had its reasons but wasn't telling anyone yet, least of all the Soviets. ■

3

NUCLEAR WEAPONS AND THE SPACE AGE

Khrushchev's boasts made for good headlines, but President Eisenhower knew better than to over-react. U-2 high-altitude spy planes had been flying over Soviet territory since 1956, and he knew the Soviets' capabilities. Yes, the United States' own ICBM program was a few years away from success, but the number of missiles that the United States had in relation to what Eisenhower knew the Soviets had was no concern for alarm. Even though newspaper headlines warned of Soviet missiles raining down on the United States, the U.S. government had many more missiles with which to annihilate Soviet and Eastern European cities.

THE ICBM

The Intercontinental Ballistic Missile is the most dangerous nuclear weapon because it flies at supersonic speeds above Earth's atmosphere. This makes it nearly impossible to shoot down. As the Soviet ICBM program moved forward, the United States missile program sped up. Within two years, as predicted by scientists to reassure Eisenhower, the United States tested its own ICBM and began a building program.

The first U.S. ICBM was called the Atlas D. It was put on alert on October 31, 1959. By the end of that year, the United States had six nuclear-tipped ICBMs. In the next three years, that number grew to 203. The Soviets were not far behind. Neither country gave up its short- or medium-range rockets. Nor did either dismantle its armies, tanks, battleships, or submarines. ICBMs, like the nuclear bombs themselves carried on the rockets, were deterrents against any attack on a friendly nation or invasion of their own countries. The arms race had gone from planes to missiles, but still neither the U.S. nor Soviet government really considered using them.

The trouble was that the missiles themselves were a lot more expensive to build than were the nuclear bombs. A new kind of arms race was about to begin. It was expensive and would take massive amounts of money and technology to keep pace with each other. This race would eventually spell the defeat of the Soviet Union and its satellite countries. But that was still nearly thirty years in the future. In the meantime, both countries used other, smaller countries as pawns in the Cold War battles for ideological supremacy.

Two U.S. Air Force captains inspect a Minuteman missile in its silo in 1964. Typically, a missile silo for a Minuteman is 80 feet (24 m) deep, 12 feet (3.7 m) wide, and is covered by a 100-ton (90.7-metric-ton) door that is blown off when the missile is launched. There were 1,000 of such missiles in six different locations around the United States by 1967.

KENNEDY LEADS A NEW RACE

In November 1960, John F. Kennedy (1917–1963) won the presidential election over Richard M. Nixon (1913–1994). Kennedy called for the youth of the nation to advance society and help other nations. The Peace Corps was developed to send Americans to help third world countries learn advanced agricultural and industrial techniques. He also called on the scientists working on the rocket program to devote energies into putting an astronaut on the Moon by the end of the decade. The scientific discoveries in rocketry would eventually help build even more powerful, accurate, and deadly ICBMs.

It was a tough task, but Kennedy's motives were to make America proud of itself and look forward after years of stagnation that had

FIRST-STRIKE FEAR

In the age of the ICBM, military planners realized that if one country could shoot its missiles before the other had a chance, then it could "win" a nuclear war before the other side could fire back. This became known as a first-strike capability. The problem with this plan was that radar could detect missile launches once they rose into the atmosphere. The response for a country under ICBM attack would be to quickly fire its own missiles, thus eliminating any first-strike success.

When submarines began carrying ICBMs, however, the response time was decreased by two-thirds, to a little more than twelve minutes. Once again, first-strike capability made winning a nuclear war possible. But even this plan had flaws when the enemy had its own fleet of submarines that were invisible to detection until it was too late. Finally, plans for winning an all-out nuclear war became rather point-less. Both countries would surely be destroyed if one fired its missiles. This idea spawned its own doctrine known as MAD—mutually assured destruction.

negatively characterized Eisenhower's presidency. Kennedy was also using this call for a new American dynamism as propaganda against the Soviet Union and Communism in general. He wanted to show the dynamics of freedom to peoples around the world.

Meanwhile, Kennedy continued to build up an already bloated American military and nuclear arsenal. He increased the size of the bomber forces and deployed newly developed land-based missiles in America's heartland. He also increased the size of America's submarine force. This was particularly important because with the newest ICBM rocket able to launch from beneath any ocean, America's strike capability became invulnerable to any Soviet strike.

Yet, as before—ever since both countries had nuclear weapons—neither was prepared to use them. Or so the United States thought until October 1962.

THE CUBAN MISSILE CRISIS

In October 1962, President Kennedy learned from spy photographs that Cuba had built missile sites on the island. Cuba is 90 miles (145 km) from mainland North America. Since the Cuban leader, Fidel Castro , had no science or rocket program of his own, Kennedy knew the missiles had to have come from the Soviets. In fact, the

President John F. Kennedy *(right)* confers with his brother and closest adviser, Attorney General Robert F. Kennedy, in the early days of the Cuban missile crisis. Robert Kennedy is generally credited with finding a diplomatic solution to the crisis.

SAM SITE
BAHIA HONDA, CUBA
23 OCTOBER 1962

CANVAS COVERED MISSILE TRAILE
IN HOLD REVETMENT

NET COVERED LAUNCHERS

BULLDOZER BURYING TANK IN REVETMENT WALL

CANVAS COVERED FRUIT SET
SURROUNDED BY VERTICAL NETTING

Aerial reconnaissance photos such as this one *(above)* provided the Kennedy administration with clear evidence that the Soviet Union was building secret nuclear missile sites in Cuba. Although Cuba's leader, Fidel Castro *(left)*, and Nikita Khrushchev appear friendly in the photo at right, Castro was infuriated when Khrushchev agreed to remove the Soviet missiles from Cuba.

photos showed missiles ready for launch, and Soviet-made equipment and personnel at these sites.

How did Cuba come to have Soviet missiles stationed on its island so close to America? In April 1961, just a year and a half before the missiles were discovered, Kennedy had approved an invasion of Cuba by Cuban exiles. This was a CIA operation planned under Eisenhower to urge the Cuban people to revolt against Castro's Communist government. The invasion proved a disaster when the CIA help that was promised never came and the Cuban-exile invaders were killed or captured as they landed at the Bay of Pigs. Castro had vowed revenge. In fact, shortly afterward, Castro began accepting money and arms from Khrushchev, including military personnel who

Most of the U.S.-trained invasion force for the Bay of Pigs operation were either killed or taken prisoner. Invasion force members were mostly Cuban exiles who had fled to the United States when Fidel Castro took power in Cuba in 1959. Operations such as the Bay of Pigs invasion and other U.S. attempts to kill or overthrow Castro led to a lasting Cuban mistrust of the United States.

helped to build and administer the rockets now stationed on the island. These medium-range missiles might have equalized the present nuclear superiority of America.

Kennedy had choices. He could order an invasion of Cuba and destroy the missile sites. This might lead to nuclear war, though. After six days, Kennedy decided to surround Cuba with U.S. Navy warships and not allow any ship into Cuba without first being searched. Kennedy knew missiles were on their way to Cuba on a Soviet ship.

This plan proved to be a good tactic. The blockade gave the two countries time to work things out diplomatically. If Khrushchev wanted to fight, war would be on his shoulders with the whole world watching. After six days, which saw Soviet naval ships moving toward Cuba, Khrushchev backed down and a compromise was made. The Soviet missiles would be removed from the

A Neptune patrol plane flies over a Soviet freighter in the Caribbean Sea at the height of the Cuban missile crisis. U.S. planes sometimes flew at tree-top level over Cuba itself in attempts to gather intelligence during the crisis. In 1992, it was revealed that the Soviets had forty-two medium-range missiles in place, guarded by 40,000 Soviet troops, that could have reached U.S. cities up to the Canadian border.

In front of congressional leaders gathered in the White House, President John F. Kennedy signs the Nuclear Test Ban Treaty in October 1963. The treaty banned nuclear weapons tests in the atmosphere, in outer space, or under water. The treaty was negotiated for eight years before each superpower was satisfied with the complex technicalities that ensured each country's interest.

island in exchange for an American promise not to invade Cuba. Later, U.S. missiles were removed from Turkey, but Kennedy never publicly admitted that this was part of the deal.

The lesson of the Cuban missile crisis forced both leaders to understand that relations had to improve. They realized that the two countries could not come within a breath of war again. By the next year, 1963, a nuclear test ban treaty was signed. Shortly thereafter, the famous "hot line" was installed between the Kremlin and the White House. This was a text-based communication network that functions twenty-four hours a day. Now the world's two superpowers could communicate directly before hostilities ever came so close to war again. ■

4

VIETNAM AND THE SALT TREATIES

Kennedy never saw the benefits of the nuclear test ban treaty. He was assassinated on November 22, 1963. Yet before that fateful day, he had made a decision to try and stop Communist aggression in Southeast Asia. After the Cuban missile crisis, Kennedy sent money, arms, and military advisers to South Vietnam. By the end of 1962,

Vice President Lyndon B. Johnson, with former first lady Jacqueline Kennedy *(right)* beside him, is sworn in as president of the United States aboard Air Force One, the presidential airplane, in Dallas, Texas, just hours after the assassination of President John F. Kennedy on November 22, 1963. In 1964, Johnson won 61 percent of the vote for the presidency, the widest margin in American history.

combat troops stood on Vietnamese soil.

Kennedy watched while more than 100 American soldiers were killed in Vietnam in 1963, while training South Vietnamese soldiers. But these soldiers could not be trained to fight effectively against the Communist Vietcong in the north. Kennedy had planned to pull any troops out after he was reelected in 1964. Of course, he never made it to the election: his assassination in Dallas, Texas, ended all plans. President Lyndon B. Johnson (1908–1973) did not follow the course that Kennedy had decided upon for Vietnam.

President Richard M. Nixon gestures toward a map of Southeast Asia during a nationwide address to the American people about the expanding U.S. role in the Vietnam War in April 1970, which led to the bombing of Cambodia. Nixon felt that a U.S. defeat in Vietnam would strengthen the Soviets and Chinese.

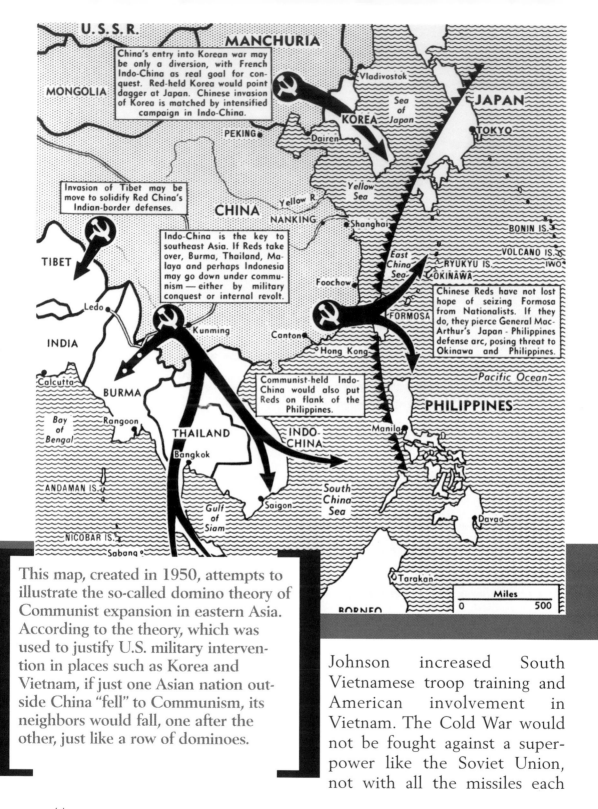

U.S.S.R.

MONGOLIA

MANCHURIA

China's entry into Korean war may be only a diversion, with French Indo-China as real goal for conquest. Red-held Korea would point dagger at Japan. Chinese invasion of Korea is matched by intensified campaign in Indo-China.

Vladivostok

JAPAN

TOKYO

Sea of Japan

KOREA

PEKING

Dairen

Invasion of Tibet may be move to solidify Red China's Indian-border defenses.

CHINA

Yellow R.

NANKING

Yellow Sea

BONIN IS.

VOLCANO IS.

TIBET

Shanghai

Indo-China is the key to southeast Asia. If Reds take over, Burma, Thailand, Malaya and perhaps Indonesia may go down under communism — either by military conquest or internal revolt.

East China Sea

RYUKYU IS.

IWO

OKINAWA

Ledo

Foochow

Chinese Reds have not lost hope of seizing Formosa from Nationalists. If they do, they pierce General MacArthur's Japan - Philippines defense arc, posing threat to Okinawa and Philippines.

Kunming

Canton

FORMOSA

INDIA

Calcutta

BURMA

Hong Kong

Pacific Ocean

Bay of Bengal

Rangoon

THAILAND

Communist-held Indo-China would also put Reds on flank of the Philippines.

PHILIPPINES

Manila

Bangkok

INDO-CHINA

ANDAMAN IS.

Gulf of Siam

Saigon

South China Sea

NICOBAR IS.

Davao

Sabang

Tarakan

Miles

0   500

BORNEO

This map, created in 1950, attempts to illustrate the so-called domino theory of Communist expansion in eastern Asia. According to the theory, which was used to justify U.S. military intervention in places such as Korea and Vietnam, if just one Asian nation outside China "fell" to Communism, its neighbors would fall, one after the other, just like a row of dominoes.

Johnson increased South Vietnamese troop training and American involvement in Vietnam. The Cold War would not be fought against a superpower like the Soviet Union, not with all the missiles each

A U.S. marine wounded in combat in South Vietnam is treated by a medic. The total number of U.S. casualties in the Vietnam War was 211,529, which includes 58,226 who were killed or missing in action, and 153,303 who were wounded. The cost and suffering of the Vietnam War led many Americans to question the U.S.'s Cold War priorities and commitments.

country had. But American leaders had decided on other ways to fight Communism.

THE VIETNAMESE QUAGMIRE

Lyndon Johnson convinced the United States that Southeast Asia was a stepping-stone for Communist aggression. The government's domino theory spread across American newspapers and into American minds. This theory was that when one country fell to Communism, it would set off the falling of each country next to it. All the countries of Southeast Asia would topple to Communism like a row of dominoes. Communism had to be stopped now, the leaders said, not when it was at America's doorstep. This policy did not include the use of nuclear weapons, of course. The Cold War battlefields of third world countries were proving grounds for ideology, not high-tech nuclear weaponry.

America's role in Vietnam quickly grew from one of giving advice and training troops to one of an all-out war against the North Vietnamese. By 1965, America's young men were being drafted for a war that would see more than 58,000 of them die in the next ten years.

Johnson and his advisers did not see the error in their policy. The South Vietnamese government and soldiers did not have the strength to battle the north. America was caught in a war that it could not win because the enemy did not fight like a regular army. Vietcong soldiers lived in caves and fought a war of attrition.

Antiwar protests in America hurt the war effort at home. America's youth were tired of the war by 1968. Richard Nixon won the presidential election that year by promising to end the war. Once in office, he actually increased the war effort for several years. Finally, when the American public had had enough, Nixon was forced to finally look for a way out. In 1975, the Vietnam War ended with the North Vietnamese crossing into the south and taking the city of Saigon just as the last American troops escaped.

A Cold War Soviet propaganda poster portrays the United States, as a beleaguered Uncle Sam being destroyed by a rain of Soviet missiles. U.S. supporters of the war in Vietnam feared that failure there would lead the Soviet Union to regard the United States as weak and indecisive.

Unlike the Korean War, which had ended with a stalemate and the south holding on to democracy, South Vietnam fell to the Communist north. America had only delayed that fall by a dozen years.

RUSSIAN CHANGE AND NUCLEAR WARHEAD ADVANCEMENT

Back in 1964, Nikita Khrushchev had lost power because of his dangerous foreign policy and the failure of the Soviet farming industry. Leonid Brezhnev (1905–1982) then became general secretary of the Communist Party and ran the country for the next seventeen years. As Brezhnev came to power, this cautious leader saw good news and bad news for the Soviet Union.

The good news was that America's involvement in Vietnam allowed the Soviets to focus on their own defense. The Soviets built a new generation of nuclear missiles that held multiple nuclear warheads. These missiles were called MIRVs, or multiple independently targeted reentry vehicles. As the missiles dropped from above the atmosphere, the warheads would launch to several different targets. Now the dangers of ICBMs became that much more serious for world peace. Of course, America had its own MIRVs and the arms buildup continued throughout the 1960s.

The bad news for the Soviets was their relationship with China; it had turned sour during the 1960s. So bad was the relationship between these two neighboring Communist nations that the Soviets amassed troops and missiles at the Chinese border. This cost the Soviet Union billions of dollars when its economy continued to struggle.

THE SALT TREATY

President Nixon's secretary of state, Henry Kissinger, believed two great superpowers could make a deal and be content with the power each held in its part of the world. Nixon agreed, and negotiations began for a Strategic Arms Limitation Talks (SALT) in 1969. SALT focused on types of missiles that could be used, their range, and how many warheads could be carried.

Both countries had enough nuclear weapons to destroy each other ten times over. The idea was for each country to stop building the weapons so that their resources could be put toward better uses, such as the economy. This suited the Soviet Union perfectly. It had wanted to decrease hostilities with the United States ever since its relationship with China had gone bad. Better yet, good relations with the United States would open its grain markets to the Soviet Union, whose agriculture industry couldn't produce enough food for its people.

In 1972, Nixon visited Moscow to bring in a new world policy of détente, or easing of strained relations. The SALT agreement was sealed.

PUTTING DÉTENTE TO THE TEST

The following year, Egypt and Syria attacked Israel on Yom Kippur, the holiest Jewish holiday. The United States airlifted much-needed supplies to the Israelis, who fought off their attackers. Brezhnev threatened to bring in forces to help the Arab states regain balance. Nixon responded by putting the country's nuclear forces on a high state of alert.

Neither the United States nor the Soviet Union wanted to battle each other over third world countries, however. They both had seen much trouble in the Middle East over the years, and this was just another phase of the same problems. Secretary of State Kissinger flew to Moscow and the Middle East to negotiate a deal. The Israelis pulled back, the Arabs were rearmed by Moscow, and détente held. The Middle East would remain a powder keg between the two superpowers for many years to come.

THE SALT II TREATY

The original SALT Treaty limited production but not deployment of nuclear missiles. Nixon had resigned from office in the face of the Watergate scandal, and Jimmy Carter was elected president in 1976. Meanwhile, Brezhnev had begun to send Soviet medium-range SS-20 missiles into its Eastern European ally countries. A Western European peace movement prevented the United States from responding with deployment of its own new Minuteman I and II rockets to European soil. It looked like Nixon's détente policy from just four years before would fail.

Jimmy Carter worked to produce a new arms limitation treaty. SALT II, like its predecessor, limited the production of new types of missiles, their range of flight, how many warheads they could carry, and where they could be stationed. The SALT II Treaty was signed between Washington and Moscow in Vienna, Austria, on June 18, 1979. The treaty never went into effect, however, because the U.S. Senate did not ratify the treaty to make the treaty a law. This was partly because the Soviet Union invaded Afghanistan late in December 1979.

Ultimately, the nonratification proved to be better for the United States than it could have imagined. The SALT II failure forced the

An Israeli soldier leads Egyptian prisoners of war to the western, or Egyptian side, of the Suez Canal during the Yom Kippur War of 1973. This was one of many battles of the Arab-Israeli conflict. President Nixon warned the Soviets during the war that he would use any option, including nuclear weapons, to protect U.S. interests in the Middle East.

Soviets to continue wasting money on weaponry as the United States itself continued to build better and more powerful missiles. In 1980, when Ronald Reagan (1911–2004) became president, the level of pressure put on the Soviet Union, its economy, society, and government, would turn the tide against the Communist superpower and bring about the end of the Cold War. ■

5

THE COLD WAR HEATS UP, THEN BURNS OUT

Republican President Ronald Reagan saw the Soviet Union as "the evil empire." Reagan blamed Communism for all the small wars happening around the world. Communists were battling democratic governments in Asia, Africa, the Caribbean Islands, and Central America. Reagan and his supporters used the threat of the Soviets and Communism around the world to establish a policy that increased the United States' military build-up, nuclear arms stockpile, and the deployment of a new missile in Europe, called the ground-launched cruise missile, or GLCM.

THE CRUISE MISSILE

The cruise missile was the next generation of nuclear missiles following the ICBM. Development had begun on it in 1945. It flew fewer than 2,000 miles (3,219 km) but lower to the ground than the ICBM. This made the missile perfect for medium range battle. Its low-flight altitude also made it invisible to enemy radar. Its deployment in Western Europe between 1979 and 1983 caused the Soviet Union to increase its own SS-20 missile program. For the first time in nearly twenty years, the term "first strike" became part of the language of nuclear war again.

A Tomahawk missile takes flight after being launched from a U.S. nuclear submarine. Tomahawks are designed to travel at very low altitudes at high speeds (up to 550 miles [885 km] per hour) for up to 1,500 miles (2,414 km) in order to deliver a large warhead.

Demonstrators tear up a poster of Vladimir Lenin in Moscow in February 1990. As the Soviet Union began to fall apart in the late 1980s, its citizens felt increasingly free to criticize the Communist system. As censorship of the media was relaxed, more information that had long been denied was available to the public and the rest of the world, exposing social and economic problems.

THE STRATEGIC DEFENSE INITIATIVE

What began as an idea for the defense of the United States and its allies served as one of the final nails in the coffin of the Soviet Union and the Cold War. Reagan and the Western allies feared the massive Soviet buildup that had taken place through the 1960s and 1970s. Even while expanding the West's buildup of arms, Reagan looked to defense. In 1983, he announced a new arms program based on defense. The Strategic Defense Initiative (SDI) would use space-based lasers and other ground-based missile systems to shield the United States from Soviet missiles.

The SDI technology was untested and would cost billions of dollars. Many U.S. scientists flat out said it wouldn't work. Critics dubbed SDI "Star Wars." Nonetheless, Reagan pushed through Congress a spending package to develop the defense system.

SOVIET CHANGE

The Soviets under Brezhnev had been installing their deadly SS-20 missiles in Eastern Europe for years. But they could not hope to match America's newer, costlier buildup. Worse, the Soviets lacked the scientific technology to build a cruise missile or develop their own SDI system. The Soviet economy was in bad shape from years of mismanagement, poor farming techniques, and industry used mostly for military hardware.

Then Brezhnev died of a heart attack in 1982, at age seventy-six. He was succeeded first by Yuri Andropov, a man not much younger, who lasted only fifteen months before he, too, died. Konstantin Chernenko succeeded Andropov, but this old-guard Soviet leader was even older and sicker. Chernenko died in March 1985, after only thirteen months in office.

The old guard of the Soviet leadership was indeed dying off and needed a new direction. They placed into office fifty-four-year-old Mikhail Gorbachev. Gorbachev (1931–) realized the Soviet Union needed radical reforming if it was going to survive. Political unrest was building in the country because of the poor economy struggling through more than a decade of failures. People waited in long lines for basic goods such as food to feed their families. The same kinds of problems were happening in the

President Ronald Reagan *(right)* and Soviet leader Mikhail Gorbachev shake hands at the White House on December 8, 1987, after signing the Nuclear Arms Reduction Treaty. Immediately after signing, the two leaders retreated to separate rooms and held press conferences. They both described the vast differences between them, but also their united effort for peace.

other eastern bloc countries because the Soviets could no longer give these countries the vast sums of money they had been giving them for more than thirty years. The Communist system inside the Soviet Union and its satellite nations was dying, and Gorbachev had reform in mind that would open the doors to freedom.

GLASNOST AND PERESTROIKA

Unable to compete against such a huge nuclear arms buildup, Gorbachev instead looked inward and tried to improve life in the Soviet Union. To Gorbachev, more weapons meant little since both superpowers had thousands of nuclear missiles apiece.

Gorbachev did more than talk about reform; he put into place a two-fold policy. First, he eliminated the secrecy of the Soviet government and made it accessible to the people. In Russian, this is called glasnost. Second, Gorbachev moved the economic system away from the central control that had been a failure for more than sixty years and put

into place economic freedom, or perestroika.

Out of this reform, Gorbachev looked to the United States and proposed to President Reagan a treaty that would cut or abolish whole systems of short- and medium-range missiles. Citizens across the West welcomed Gorbachev's style and reforms, and this arms-reduction offer. After his initial skepticism, Reagan, too, saw the seriousness of the Soviet leader's offer.

Within a year, Gorbachev went even further and proposed eliminating in Europe every single short- and medium-range missile if the United States would do the same—called the "zero-zero" agreement. The Intermediate-Range Nuclear Force Treaty took force in 1987. The Cold War was basically over. The face-off between East and West ended with not a war, but

Germans began dismantling the Berlin Wall in November 1989. The wall, which had divided the city of Berlin into western (democratic) and eastern (Communist) sectors since the early 1960s, was perhaps the most famous symbol of the Cold War division of Europe. Just months later, authorities in Bucharest, Romania, authorized the removal of the huge statue of Lenin *(inset)* that had stood in front of the government house there for decades.

peace and a growing unity based on the business of providing for the people of a nation.

THE COLLAPSE OF EASTERN EUROPEAN COMMUNISM

In 1986, Gorbachev won an election over conservative opponents. He instituted further changes that were revolutionary to Soviet politics: free elections of local leaders and even the Supreme Soviet, or legislature.

These same reforms were taking place in the Soviet satellite nations: Czechoslovakia, East Germany, Hungary, Poland, and Romania. In quick succession in 1989, each of these countries saw mass demonstrations. The people wanted change, and the governments mostly moved aside peacefully. In November 1989, the Berlin Wall came down.

Then, in 1990, Gorbachev took away the special privileges of the Communist Party. He told the party that it would have to compete with other parties in the future for power. Almost immediately, many republics of the Soviet Union rose up in defiance and demanded freedom. The Soviet Union was powerless in stopping this action. Gorbachev watched the quick succession of republics and made it clear to all the leaders that there was no turning back. Communism was over in this part of the world. The Cold War was dead. Freedom had won over rule by terror. By 1991, the Soviet Union had ceased to exist.

AFTER THE COLD WAR

The Cold War may be over, but nuclear weapons remain in the world. In fact, at least seven nations own nuclear weapons, including India, Pakistan, and North Korea. India and Pakistan have had their own cold war going for many years, sometimes bubbling over to conventional arms battles across their borders.

The United States and the former Soviet Union kept each other honest about using nuclear weapons because of their destructive force. The countries never went to war because they understood that neither could survive such an attack. Do the other nations hold that same regard for war and life? So far the world has seen this to be true. The only way for the human race to survive is to not make the mistake of using nuclear weapons to solve its problems. ■

[GLOSSARY]

ally A friendly person or country who has a pact to help another country or group.

arms race A term used by government and media to describe the buildup of military arms and nuclear weapons by the United States and the Soviet Union.

Bolsheviks The name for the Communist organization that overthrew Czar Nicholas II of Russia during the 1917 Russian Revolution.

capitalism An economic system in which individuals or private corporations own the means of business and industry.

Cold War A period in twentieth-century history during which the Soviet Union and the United States built up huge armies and weapons stockpiles but never went to war against each other.

Communism A political system under which the government controls business and industry. Pure Communism occurs when all people live in a classless society. Communism as practiced by the Soviets and other twentieth-century governments used terror and military rule to keep people from revolting.

cruise missile A low-flying and slow missile that is invisible to enemy radar.

fission The splitting of atoms.

fusion The combining of atoms.

glasnost A Soviet political system of openness and public accountability begun by Mikhail Gorbachev in 1985.

hydrogen bomb A nuclear bomb using the energy of atoms that combine rather than split to create a much more deadly explosion than ordinary nuclear bombs that rely on fission.

intercontinental ballistic missile (ICBM) A missile that has a range of more than 5,500 miles (8,851 km) and can fly out of the atmosphere to reach a distant continent.

Manhattan Project The U.S. scientific project to build the first atomic bomb.

missile A rocket shot from the ground, the air, or beneath the sea for attack purposes.

nuclear bomb An explosive device using highly radioactive material—usually plutonium—to create a blast that destroys life and structures for miles around.

perestroika The Soviet program of economic reform and freedom begun by Mikhail Gorbachev in 1985.

plutonium A by-product of uranium whose atoms have been split. Plutonium is much more radioactive than uranium and therefore a good source of weapons-grade radioactive material.

revolution An event that sees people overtaking one system of government for another, for example overthrowing a king or dictator to hand power over to the people.

Star Wars A term used by the media to describe the weapons defense system pushed by Ronald Reagan's Strategic Defense Initiative (SDI) in 1983.

Strategic Defense Initiative (SDI) A laser defense system to be based in orbit around Earth to destroy missiles.

Truman Doctrine A policy put forward by President Harry S. Truman in 1947, stating that the United States would assist any people or government trying to fight against a power within or outside its country that was trying to oppress its people.

United Nations Security Council One of the major bodies of the United Nations, established on October 24, 1945. The five victors of World War II—the United States, Great Britain, France, China, and the Soviet Union—are the five permanent members of the council with veto power, while ten other countries can serve two-year terms. Its main function is to maintain international peace.

uranium A natural element found in rock that is radioactive and is used for atomic energy and to make nuclear weapons material.

[FOR MORE INFORMATION]

Arms Control Association
1150 Connecticut Avenue NW, Suite 620
Washington, DC 20036
Web site: http://www.armscontrol.org

Center for Nonproliferation Studies
460 Pierce Street
Monterey, CA 93940
e-mail: cns@miis.edu
Web site: http://cns.miis.edu

NATO Headquarters
Blvd Leopold III
1110 Brussels, Belgium
e-mail: natodoc@hq.nato.int

UN Headquarters
First Avenue at 46th Street
New York, NY 10017
Web site: http://www.un.org/english

WEB SITES

Due to the changing nature of Internet links, the Rosen Publishing
Group, Inc., has developed an on-line list of Web sites related to the
subject of this book. This site is updated regularly. Please use this link
to access the list:

http://www.rosenlinks.com/lwmd/nwcw

[FOR FURTHER]

READING

Cheney, Glenn Alan. *Nuclear Proliferation: The Problems and Possibilities*. New York: Franklin Watts, 1999.

Dudley, William, ed. *The Cold War (Opposing Viewpoints)*. San Diego: Greenhaven, 1992.

Kraljic, Matthew A., ed. *The Breakup of Communism: The Soviet Union and Eastern Europe*. New York: H. W. Wilson, 1993.

Watson, William E. *The Collapse of Communism in the Soviet Union*. Westport, CT: Greenwood Press, 1998.

Winkler, Allan M. *The Cold War: A History in Documents*. New York: Oxford University Press, 2000.

[BIBLIOGRAPHY]

Constable, George, ed. *Time Frame AD 1950–1990: The Nuclear Age*. New York: Time, Inc. Books, 1990.

Dudley, William, ed. *The Cold War (Opposing Viewpoints)*. San Diego: Greenhaven, 1992.

Gates, Robert M. *From the Shadows: The Ultimate Insider's Story of Five Presidents and How They Won the Cold War*. New York: Simon & Schuster, 1996.

Kissinger, Henry. *Diplomacy*. New York: Simon & Schuster, 1994.

Kort, Michael G. *The Cold War*. Brookfield, CT: Millbrook Press, 1994.

Murphy, David E., Sergei A. Kondrashev, and George Bailey. *Battle Ground Berlin: CIA vs. KGB in the Cold War*. New Haven, CT: Yale University Press, 1997.

Warren, James A. *Cold War: The American Crusade Against World Communism 1945–1991* New York: Lothrop, Lee & Shepard, 1996.

Watson, William E. *The Collapse of Communism in the Soviet Union*. Westport, CT: Greenwood Press, 1998.

Winkler, Allan M. *The Cold War: A History in Documents*. New York: Oxford University Press, 2000.

[INDEX]

ABOUT THE AUTHOR

Mark Beyer is the author of more than a dozen books on history, government, social sciences, and sports, as well as biographies. He has edited anthologies of nonfiction literature on both world wars. He is also a fiction author and a literary critic whose column, "Cover to Cover," appears in the *Tampa Tribune's Flair* magazine. You can read some of those reviews at his Web site, www.Bibliogrind.com.

PHOTO CREDITS

Cover, pp. 7, 38 (top), 41 © Corbis; pp. 4–5, 11, 13, 17, 18-19, 21, 23, 24, 26–27, 29, 43, 44, 53 © Bettmann/Corbis; pp. 8–9 © Yevgeny Khaldei/Corbis; p. 10 © Hulton-Deutsch Collection/Corbis; p. 15 © Bradley Smith/Corbis; pp. 25, 31, 33, 40, 49, 54–55 Getty Images; pp. 34, 45, 51 Time Life Pictures/Getty Images; pp. 37, 50, 55 (inset) © AP/Wide World Photos; p. 38 (bottom) © TASS/Sovfoto; pp. 39, 46 © Sovfoto/Eastfoto.

Designer: Evelyn Horovicz; Editor: Leigh Ann Cobb; Layout: Thomas Forget; Photo Researcher: Rebecca Anguin-Cohen